Disclaimer:

While the author hopes that this book will be valuable and helpful for you or your business, they cannot make any guarantee that the steps within are appropriate for your situation, or guarantee increase in profits or any other improvements as a result of implementing steps or ideas from within this book.

All information is accurate at the time of writing, and to the authors knowledge, however no liability will be accepted for any inaccuracies that may accidentally occur.

You carry out or implement any advice within this book entirely at your own risk.

Advice and steps within this book should not be seen as a substitute for seeking legal or professional advice or help.

Introduction

The book you are about to read may seem like a strange idea - a book on reading a book!

So many people read business and personal development books, get an initial spark of inspiration, and then never really do anything, forgetting about the book they've read and letting it gather dust.

This is a book full of techniques, hints and tips to help you get the most from the non-fiction books you read - to get you REALLY trying the ideas and making changes to your business.

Perhaps you have started your business, and looking for books to discover ideas to improve your business? Or you have been in your current role for a while and decided to start reading business related books? Or you enjoy reading and insights from particular authors?

I've found reading non-fiction books can make a difference - and I hope this book helps give you the push and some techniques to use ideas from the books you have read to take your business forward.

And while this may sound like a strange idea for a book - I also hope that by the end of this book you won't find it so strange - and that you've learned some new ways to look at and try ideas you read.

What qualifies me to write this book? As well as reading and trying the ideas from various books I've read, since 2019 I've also organised a business book club - which you can find at **www.booksandnetworking.co.uk**

I hope you enjoy reading this book - and find it valuable. I'd love to hear how you get on trying the ideas within its pages - you can contact me via e-mail at: **simon@libraryplayer.co.uk**

Simon Pittman
9th June 2023

Getting Started

What is a business book?

In 2019, after seeing lots of "what is everyone reading at the moment" posts, I decided to create a Facebook group where everyone's book recommendations could be gathered together and discussed, and hopefully help people discover new books!

The group has grown since then, with over 200 members, and regular networking events in Aberdeen.

This did get me thinking - what exactly is a business book?

For example - shortly after creating the group I was asked if personal development books counted and could be included - and the answer to this is yes! This also led me to updating the group description to clarify this.

There are also autobiographies and books that don't contain practical steps, and are more inspirational - these count too, especially if they help someone's work or business.

I have lots of nonfiction books - do books that cover industry specific topics count? A more difficult one to answer - although something covered in more detail later on in this chapter!

How about books that indirectly help your work or business, or perhaps read not for the ideas, and for the joy of reading?

Even though we often talk about "business" books - not everyone owns a business. Many people work as employees, or have part-time jobs to support their business - and still like to read non-fiction.

And is the format of a book important? Whether it's a paperback, Kindle or audio book, it still counts.

If it's a non-fiction book that helps your work or business, then I'd consider it a business book.

Everyone is different - some may only consider books that you find the "Business" section of Waterstones or the local library to count, however I believe you can find gems in other book categories too.

I've even pushed the boundaries even further from time to time - and started encouraging people to share other forms of written content within the group (e.g. blog posts they have written, magazines, etc.) - although at the moment these are only in specific posts.

What do you think? What is your definition of a business book?

You won't see instant results from any book you read. And you definitely won't "get rich quick"!

Sceptical about reading business books?

Business (and non-fiction in general) books are a great way to help you improve and grow your business - from learning new skills, discovering tips, inspiration and ideas you may not have considering trying.

Many people may not be sure about reading business books - for a variety of reasons. These can include...

- Thinking that all books in that category are rubbish.
- Tried reading business books and put off by a few bad ones.
- Not a fan of the style of writing in many books.
- Stereotype of self help gurus full of false promises.
- Believing they know everything and there is nothing the books can help with.
- Being "too busy" and not having the time to read.
- Not getting anything from the books you read.
- Low quality books full of sales pitches.

All these reasons to be unsure and reluctant to read business books are perfectly valid - and hopefully this section will address many of them.

First of all - can business books really make a difference to your business? Yes - I believe so - especially if you find the right books for you and your business.

However if you are not getting anything from a book you are reading at the moment or finding it difficult to complete, then put that particular book away and find something else to read.

Why read business books?

- Learning.
- Inspiration.
- Motivation.
- Improve.
- New skills.
- Interest.

Sit down - consider what you would like help with in your business, and the skills you would like to learn, and which categories of books you like (or would like to) read.

Remember - not all books have a "cheerleader style" or full of style over substance or make false promises - don't let one or two terrible books put you off.

And you don't have to rush reading a book so you can quickly move on to the next one - take your time reading the book, reflecting and trying the steps.

If you don't have time to read, or worried about adding extra time in your schedule, consider reading business/personal development books as part of your working day.

There are different options available for reading - audiobooks, ebooks, paperback - and if you don't want to read a book look for other forms of written (or business related) content, e.g. blog posts, podcasts, videos, magazines, trade publications, etc.

When finding ideas for books to read, or considering reading a particular book - look at the reviews. Be aware that some reviews may be written by an author's clients or their competitors - so it's worth looking for reviews outside of book selling websites, e.g. blog posts (I regularly post book reviews on my LinkedIn profile).

Look at books other people are recommending - either your friends, contacts or within my own book group.

No business book is a "magic wand" that fixes all your problems - especially if you don't try any of the steps or just put the book away and then forget about it.

Read books help with a particular area of your business, or specific to your industry (in my case that would be computer books).

On a similar note - don't just look in the Business section of bookstores - you'll find excellent non-fiction books to help your business in many other categories and areas.

Don't feel like you have to constantly read new books or hundred of books a year - try a few favourites that you go back and re-read.

Have any business owners you like (e.g. LinkedIn connections, well-known authors, etc.)? Or any celebrity business owners? Try reading their books - e.g. their autobiographies.

If you don't want to invest too much money in business books, then charity shops and libraries are a great place for finding and reading books at a low price or free (and some libraries have ebooks available that you can download for free).

If you have found a book you like the look of, and still not sure, visit the author's website. They often have sample chapters, blog posts and some cases even free downloads - so you can see their style of writing (and whether their books could help you) before purchasing.

My final tip if you are not sure about reading business books - don't think about them as "business books". In particular, don't consider them books that are a chore and that you have to read just for the sake of reading (if this is the case, are you reading the right business books).

There are many great business and non-fiction books out there - consider the reasons you might want to read and what you would like to improve or the skills you would like to learn.

Find the right books for you - you may enjoy reading different books every week, or have one of two favourites.

Years ago if anyone said "business books" I would have groaned - and had many of the same thoughts I mentioned at the start of this post. However I came across a few really great books, which changed my views on business/personal development books.

I've discovered many books since that I always go back to and re-read - and its always great discovering ideas for new books to read, and seeing what everyone else is reading too.

The best way to start reading is to actually start! Pick up a book and read one or two pages!

Do computer books count?

When friends where reading books (usually fiction) and asking what I was reading at the moment - I would always be cheeky and ask: **do computer books count?**

At the time, I was reading a lot of them! Some of them I just enjoyed reading, others I read to gain new knowledge. It's helped me learn a lot of my skills. My reply was always in humour, and they would often respond that it didn't count!

However, now that I read a lot of business books (and even have a Facebook group to discuss them, and planned networking meetings) the question has a new meaning - this time in relation to whether they count as a business book.

While I use do computer books count here - it could apply to other things - for example recipe books, books on finance, etc.

And I would say **YES they do count!**

While not strictly a business book (in that it would be in a separate category in the local bookstore or library) - if a book helps your work or business in any way, then I'd say yes - it counts as a business book.

Those books help improve your work or business, or inspire you with new ideas. A chef or baker could be inspired by a recipe book, an accountant could keep up-to-date with books on finance, authors read books on writing, etc.

The most important thing is that you learn from these books, carry out the steps, revisit sections, etc. (although a computer book still doesn't count if it's in response to a question on fictional books)!

What makes a good business book?

Everyone is different - so what makes a good book for me may be something completely for you - as long as you are getting something from that book (even just the enjoyment of reading it) that is the most important thing.

So what makes a good business book for me?

- Practical and realistic steps that can be carried out. I'm not a fan of books from "experts" or "consultants" where they skip on details, because they want you to hire them!

- I'd love to visit an author's website, and sign up for their newsletter - but only because I've got something from the book, and not because I need to do so to carry out the steps.

- Makes me want to re-read the entire book, or revisit chapters.

- The author may be a celebrity or well-known, however I've not heard of them - and they don't assume their reader has.

- Doesn't talk down to the reader, e.g. with an "I know everything" attitude or is snobbery.

- Isn't filled with inspirational quotes and not much else.

- Easy to read and follow.

- No false promises. I am very suspicious of books that promise I will become a millionaire within a few hours!

- Doesn't try to use jargon or to be clever.

- Only need to read one book - and not buy every book in the series so I can actually follow the steps (I'll buy your other books because I like the one I'm currently reading).

- Most importantly - I actually get something from reading the book. Whether that is ideas to try, or changes I can make to my business.

What makes a good business (or non-fiction book) for you?

How reading books is similar to Netflix!

Yes - that is an unusual headline - **how can reading a business or personal development book be similar to watching Netflix?**

(And for those that prefer Amazon Prime, Paramount+, Disney+ or the other services - the same principle applies!)

- **Once you start reading, the amount of time it takes to read the book doesn't seem that long.** Sometimes you may even revisit chapters (or rewatch your favourite episodes), fast forward, rewind, stop and take a break, etc.

- **If you are not getting anything from it, you can stop!** When you are a few episodes into a new Netflix show, and you are not enjoying it, you can stop - the same principle applies to reading. If you are not getting anything from the book, finding it a chore to read or not enjoying it, stop and read something else instead.

- **No matter how many tasks you have in your life, how much work you have to do, all your other priorities - you always find time to watch those boxsets!** It's like having a time machine sometimes - just as you can make time to watch those shows you love, you can also find the time to read those books.

- **It's a great talking point - tell your friends, family and the entire world!** OK, maybe some people won't be interested in the non-fiction books you are reading - unless they are other business owners!

There are some ways where it's very different - for example - you shouldn't "binge read" the business book and move quickly to the next one - take your time and read it properly - stop and reflect - take notes - carry out all those actions you say you will.

While learning new skills and discovering new ideas, reading business or personal development books should still be something you enjoy!

Myths around business books

When you hear the words "business books" - what are your first thoughts?

Ideas for books to read that will help your business, something inspirational, potential new ideas to try, self-help or practical?

Sometimes it may create pictures in your mind of cheesy cheerleader style books, full of nothing but inspirational quotes, buzzwords and not much else.

You may even hear the words "business books" and "personal development" and groan. And when I started my business 11 years ago I had the same perceptions around business books.

Here are some of the myths I've come across around business books, along with some hints and tips...

- **Business books don't necessarily mean business books.** It's not always about reading the books found in the "Business" section of a bookstore.

- **You have nothing to learn, or think "yeah, right, already know everything"** - whatever your business or area of expertise, there is always something new to learn - whether that's new ideas, tools, techniques, marketing or the business side of things.

- **"Just inspirational quotes", etc.** - some people love these style of books, however they are not for everyone, and most business books are not like this.

- **Don't let one bad book put you off.** You may have read a business book you didn't enjoy reading, or didn't really get anything from - however it is worth having a look at other books and authors.

- **You are "too busy" or "don't have time to read business books"** - listen to audiobooks while you work, or just read a few pages a day - you'll soon find you are reading (or listening!) to the entire book in no time. And it can be better to take your time, rather than rushing and trying to read an entire book within a few days.

- **You don't have to read 52 books a year.** Sometimes reading one or two really good business books, re-reading books/chapters and actually trying ideas, can be more effective then reading lots of books and then forgetting them.

- **"Books are too expensive"** - a lot of books are comparable to other non-fiction books out there - and you can also find many books second hand at lower prices, sample chapters/blogs on author's websites or even available to borrow at local libraries.

- **Think you can do better? Write your own book!** I'm being serious here - share your knowledge and skills - what do you wish you'd known when you started your business? What hints and tips can you share with people in your industry?

- **Business books "won't make a difference" or are a "waste of time"** - non-fiction books are not a magic solution that will solve all your problems overnight or an alternative to seeking professional help. Trying the steps and ideas in any book will take time before you see the results.

If you are not sure about reading business books - don't think about them as business books - they are non-fiction books.

Find the right book for you. You'll soon find your favourite authors, style of writing, etc.

It's not reading a book just for the sake of reading it either. Try new books - read books that look like something of interest - or can help improve a particular area of your business. Read the author's blog posts, sample pages, etc. if you are unsure whether it's a book for you.

Not essential

This may seem like a radical thing for me to say (especially in a book about reading business books!) - however:

You don't have to read business books. It's not essential!

I've met business owners who have been in business for 30+ years, and never read a single business book. It's not essential to your business survival.

However, reading non-fiction books is great for learning new ideas, finding inspiration, picking up new skills, etc. - so it's something I do encourage. And if can make a big difference to your business or life - especially when you read the right books.

What I'm saying is - read for the right reasons - whether to learn, or just for the joy of reading. Don't read a book because you feel you have to, it feels like the current "big thing", or because a business coach has told you to.

If it feels like a chore, or something you aren't really getting anything from - stop! Read something else. Try something different - e.g. listening to podcasts, or attending courses at your local college.

Don't let one book put you off. Try different authors, styles, formats, etc.

What's so exciting about business books?

A few years ago I got a message from someone, talking about my book group on Facebook, asking "what is my interest in books?"

Reading non-fiction really can make a difference - especially when you actually try ideas and steps within their pages (rather than just reading once and letting the book gather dust).

Here's why reading business (and non-fiction) books is so exciting...

- **New skills.** Whether a practical "how to" book (e.g. the For Dummies series), or to improve a particular area of a business (e.g. marketing).

- **Inspirational.** Whether designed to motivate, sharing real world experiences, or learning about other people's journeys.

- **Improve a particular aspect or area of your life.**

- **Interesting.** You just find the book interesting, or enjoy reading - even if it doesn't directly benefit your business.

- **Learn how others have done it.** Other people's stories on how they have started, grown or improved their business can help with your own work and journey.

- **Work on a particular part of your life (e.g. communication).** However, remember that reading non-fiction is not a substitute for seeking professional help!

- **New ideas to try in your work or business.**

- **Save time and/or money.** Why invest in an expensive course when a book (sometimes by the same person who delivers that training) can be more cost effective.

Anything you would add? How have non-fiction books made a difference to your work or business? Any particular books that have stood out and had an impact, or any particular favourites?

You don't have to read 52 books a year, or spend lots of money on books - you can borrow books from libraries, find some excellent books in charity shops, or check out an author's website.

Business books don't necessarily have to be business books. Any category of book that helps your work - and it doesn't just have to be what you find in the "business" category in bookstores. There is so much potential.

Take your time, actually read, reread and try ideas. More effective to read one book a year, and do something, then read lots, and never taking action.

If you find reading something you dread, or not sure where to start - pick your favourite business leader, author or someone who inspires you - and start by reading their book.

Reading a book and not really getting anything from the book, and don't like the thought of reading another page? Stop! Take a break, or find a different book to read - although don't let one book put you off reading the many other books that are out there.

While non-fiction books are great for new skills, making a difference, and inspiration - remember they are not a "magic wand" or instant solution that will magically solve your problems. If your business is really struggling, or you are at a point where you are desperate - look for professional advice, help and support - rather than relying on a book to fix things.

Many books out there, covering different topics (or the same topics in different ways), by a wide range of authors - there is something for everyone - even if "you don't read business books"!

Finding & Purchasing

Finding the right business book

It can sometimes be difficult to choose the right book to read - you may not be sure where to start or which book to start reading. **Here are some ideas to help you pick and choose the books to read...**

- Recommendations from other people.

- Any areas of your business you are looking to work on?

- Read pages from different books, and find one where you like the style of writing and books that can help you.

- Look in your local library for different books - you can borrow them, and discover ideas for great books to read.

- Many libraries also have ebooks and other business resources available to borrow and download for free too.

- Everyone is different - a style of writing in one book may not be for you, so don't let one bad business book put you off.

- Check out author's blog posts, etc. as well.

- Remember all categories of non-fiction books count - and not just ones in the Business section of your bookstore!

- Rather than asking "which book should I read" instead ask "what am I looking for help with in my business?"

- Don't dismiss or rule out a book because you "know everything" –still potential insights, ideas and inspiration.

- Are there local authors in your area, whose books you may be interested in reading?

- You don't have to read a new book every time! Revisit previous books you have read - re-read particular chapters.

Stop buying books! Look at your bookcase - when was the last time you reread any of the books you already have (even just one page)?

You don't have to read new books all the time!

One tip I share throughout these pages is that you don't always have to read a new book.

In fact, it can be a good thing to go back and revisit and re-read books you previously read (although it's still an excellent idea to read and look at new books too).

It's tempting - and I've seen many - just read new books every time, or read a book, promise to try the ideas, and just forget about them.

Even reading a book, and saying it didn't really help or do anything for them - because they didn't really take their time and do anything about it - instead choosing to read book after book after book.

Quality over quantity - you could read only one book this year, make one or two changes that make a BIG difference - this is more effective than constantly reading book after book, and never really stopping to do anything about it.

So instead of reading a new book, look at your bookcase and revisit some of the past books you have read...

- Re-read one page or a chapter - especially if you feel "you don't have time" to re-read that book.
- Perhaps the first time round you didn't take notes or try the exercises or steps - rereading a book is a great opportunity to take your time to do this.
- If you have previously tried and followed the steps - revisiting the book or particular sections is a great opportunity to see if you come across something new, steps you didn't try out, or something else you'd try now upon reflection.

- Remember to visit the author's website too, and follow them on social media - they often post extra resources or content that can also help you.

- Recently read another book by the same author? It's a great opportunity to go back and revisit their books you have previously read.

- Previously disagreed or struggled with a particular section of the book? Revisit those parts again - now you have more time to focus on those sections, and you may understand them differently a second time round.

- Have you previously read a book, promised you'd take action, and then forgot about it or didn't do anything? Or read a book, didn't feel it really worked and didn't follow the steps? It's a great opportunity to go back and give them a try.

It's not a sprint. You don't need to read (or re-read) books as quickly as possible. Take your time. Actually understand what is written within the book. Reflect on each page or chapter.

And if you decide to just re-read one page or revisit a particular part of the book - that's a great thing to do too. You can focus on what is covered, trying the steps, etc. rather than trying everything within the full book.

A theme throughout this book - less is more! Read a few pages. Pick one or two favourite books. Try one or two ideas at a time.

Best places to find & purchase books

A few years ago, I asked on my Facebook group where everyone purchases their books from! Some excellent ideas and places, and I've included some of these in the list below…

- **New from your local bookstore or online.** If you can't find books within a local store - remember to ask the staff as often they can order them in for you.
- **The "new and used" section on Amazon** - you can often find books for 1p plus postage!
- **Some newsagents**, e.g. WH Smiths also sell books.
- **Charity shops are a great place.** I've found quite a few excellent books in charity shops - as have others in the group.
- **Car boot sales.**
- **Local libraries often sell withdrawn books.**
- **And of course you can borrow books from your local library.** This is a great way to discover new books, or read books if you can't afford them. It's also worth checking out the other resources they may have to help your business too.
- **When searching Amazon or other online stores, try different keywords and mis-spellings.** You can sometimes find separate listings at an excellent price, hidden away due to the title or author being misspelled!
- **Direct from the author's website.**
- **Authors often post samples, sections/samples of their books and extra content on their website or blogs.**

And remember - if you purchase a book - whether it's new or a charity shop find, don't just leave it on your bookcase or at the side, actually read it!

Charity shops

I've found a number of excellent business books in local charity shops - some that have proven to be really valuable for my business.

Some of the books are pre-loved (with folded pages, notes written, etc.) while others are in almost new condition.

Most charity shops are not the dusty, untidy places full of tacky items that are often the stereotype that people imagine.

Some have a small selection, a few shops will have a really large selection of books - and some even have their own bookshops (e.g. in Aberdeen there is an Oxfam bookshop and the VSA bookshop).

Over time you'll find you have a few favourite charity shops that you like to visit - in fact shops that you will make a point of travelling to visit rather than just when you are going past!

Here are some hints and tips for finding business (or personal development or any other non-fiction) books in charity shops...

- **Look in different and other sections.** Sometimes staff end up putting books in the wrong place - I've previously found "Eat That Frog" and "4 Hour Work Week" in the Comedy section as the staff had assumed it was a comedy book based on the title/cover (rather than a business book).
- **Negotiate price.** Some shops are happy for you to do this, others dislike, so be careful and use discretion. Remember charity shops are trying to raise as much money as possible for their charities. Worth trying if you are a regular customer, or buying multiple items (e.g. where the total is £12 asking if it can be rounded to £10).

- **Don't forget the reduced section.** Some shops have a clearance/reduction/half price section so worth checking out.

- **If a book seems worn or much loved - don't necessarily let that put you off.** Especially if the book is 50p or £1. If a book is not in great condition, also worth bringing to the attention to the shop staff, you may be able to get the book at a reduced price!

- **Don't rule out previous editions of books, older books from over 5 years ago, etc.** - they may still be more relevant then you realise. And there may not be that much difference between the edition in the shop and later editions.

- **You may be able to find the books at lower prices online, or be able to buy a new copy of the book at a similar price.** You could always use this as an opportunity to negotiate on the price.

- **It's a great opportunity to try books that you may not have considered reading** - especially when 50p or £1!

- **Start a conversation with shop staff** - smile, be friendly, even say "hello" as you walk in. Especially when you visit often - being friendly (and staff remembering/recognising you) can be handy with the other tips here.

- **Even if a shop doesn't have anything at the moment - they could in the future.** So it's worth visiting regularly, each time you are passing, etc.

- **When you buy a book, why not add a post on Twitter, LinkedIn and/or Facebook** - and mention the charity shop?

- **If there is something you are looking for that you can't see - it's worth asking the staff.** If they have lots of stuff donated, so they may still have items at the back of the shop.

- **On a similar note, if you find a book you like, it may be worth asking if they have any more similar books, books by the same author, etc.** Sometimes people donate a bunch of books, and it takes the shop a while to sort out - so again they may be some more books at the back of the shop.

Getting books for free!

I'm sometimes asked (or see asked within my book group on Facebook) where books can be read or found for free. Authors (and publishers, etc.) have bills to pay - however there can be various reasons for wishing to get a book for free or very low cost.

Where can you find free non-fiction books?

- **Borrow from local libraries.** If you can't find a book or category of book, ask library staff, they may get the book if there is enough interest or point you towards similar books.

- **Some libraries have great reference/business sections too.**

- **A lot of libraries now have many excellent free online resources and ebooks that you can access from home and download for free** if you are a member of the library.

- **Authors websites** - many authors include sample chapters from their books that you can read free (great way to determine if book worth purchasing). There are also blog posts (some of which may also appear in their books) and other resources worth checking out too.

- **Facebook groups, connecting with authors on LinkedIn or their other online communities** - sometimes authors offer free book offers (particularly Kindle versions)

- **Keep an eye out on their Amazon pages** - on a similar note to the previous point, authors sometimes make Kindle editions of their books available for free for a few days.

- **Kindle Unlimited and/or Audible Subscriptions** - plus you may find other similar services too - while not strictly free (as you pay a subscription)

- **Ask your friends or business contacts if they can lend you their copy**, or if they have brought a new edition if you can have their copy of the previous edition.

- **Attend workshops or events organised by authors or their companies** - either locally or online - they sometimes offer free copies of their books to delegates (although don't just attend expecting something for free!)
- **Something I frequently mention - you don't always need to read new books.** Revisit/reread books you already have.

Keep in mind with all the above points (and in general): smile - engage - and don't expect or demand something for free. You are more likely to read books or other resources for free if you are not selfish and do something solely for that reason.

When looking at the above methods and ways - take your time - explore the websites and resources properly - you'll discover other new things along the way too, and appreciate what you are looking for much more.

Don't undervalue any free resources you access or read. If you get a copy of a book for free - take the time to actually read them! Send the author a note or short message too, thanking them for the free copy, and letting them know what you got or learned from the book, and how it made a difference.

As I'm talking about finding books to read for free, DO NOT even think of using pirate websites or trying to access pirated copies of digital books. Not only can this cause all sorts of problems, it could damage your own reputation.

Remember - authors have bills to pay too. If you can afford to purchase a copy of their book, then please do so.

One final note: there are various low cost options - e.g. charity shops, used copies from Amazon sellers, etc. And many books can be found new at very low prices these days - often for the same price as a week's worth of coffee from large coffee chains!

Ghost written books

I'm sure this is a topic that could be debated - books that are ghost-written (i.e. someone else has written the book for the author).

This may not be an issue for you (although it can still be fun reading this section and spotting clues) - and it can be difficult to tell if a book is ghost-written - however, there can be a few clues...

- If the author is a "celebrity" or well-known, can you really imagine them sitting down for hours and writing a book?

- When a book has a co-author, there's a good chance the co-author have actually written most or the entire book.

- Acknowledgements page may include something along the lines of "I'd like to thank Joe Bloggs for helping share my story" - in this example Joe Bloggs may be a ghost-writer (if in doubt, you can Google the name!).

- Writing styles change from each book the author releases.

- Authors openly acknowledge they work with a ghost-writer.

- Ghost-writer may have mentioned on their website or LinkedIn profile who they work with - although this is rare.

There's no guarantee - authors are not obliged to acknowledge ghost writers (after all, the point is to present the idea someone has written the book themselves).

Don't let the fact a book is ghost-written put you off - or you worry too much that it prevents you from enjoying the books you read!

Ghost-written can mean different things - sometimes a ghost-writer will have just a title, other times they may have a more detailed outline, and on other occasions it's pretty much complete, or they have detailed notes, and they just have to make improvements!

Book summary apps

You may have seen these advertised on TV or online - book summary apps. Blinkist is probably the most well-known one.

The idea is that instead of having to read the entire book, these apps or services will provide a short summary of the book's ideas, saving you time.

It's up to you whether you choose to use any of these - personally I'm not a fan. And there's some debate whether you'll get the full context of a book's ideas using these services (although there's also an argument that if you like the ideas, it will encourage you to check out the actual book).

However, a lot of these services do not pay the original authors.

As the summaries are presented as reviews, and summaries of the ideas, rather than the original work, they are not using any copyrighted material and therefore do not have to pay the authors, publishers, etc.

You may feel this is not an issue - however imagine if you sold products. And someone sold copycat versions of your products (i.e. your ideas) and profited from them, without ever paying you a single penny. Is this really any different? Even if this example doesn't apply to you - I'm sure you may have friends or know people who sell craft products, etc. Where do you draw the line?

There are a number of book summary services and apps, and a few of them do involve and pay the original authors - so it may be worth looking into these (although checking that they do genuinely pay the original authors)!

Book Reviews

A great way to decide whether to read a book is to look at the reviews.

However, be careful when looking at reviews for business books...

- A lot of reviews may be written by the author's coaching clients. In some cases, they may have written the reviews for them (you'll notice some reviews are similarly worded).

- Some authors even encourage bad reviews to be left on their competitors books.

- Author's buying reviews - doesn't necessarily mean paying money for someone to write a review, it can also be an incentive, e.g. free/discounted copies of the book (or other items) in exchange for a review. This is against Amazon's terms and conditions!

- Family, friends, etc. leaving reviews.

If you've ever wondered why some books you didn't really enjoy reading seem to have lots of great reviews - the above reasons are probably why!

(Saying that, it could also be that you didn't enjoy the book - or its ideas didn't connect with you - this is perfectly normal, and everyone's different.)

Every author gets one star reviews at some point. Look at every best-selling and well-known book - most have great reviews, however you'll also see less favourable reviews. I'd be more suspicious if a book just had hundreds of five star reviews, and no lower ratings.

You may see strange or suspicious patterns of behaviour when looking at reviews - for example a large number of reviews from the same date, reviews that don't match the description of the book, etc.

Look at the reviews - however be aware of what I've mentioned in this section when using reviews to make a decision.

Use reviews alongside the "Look Inside" feature, to look at a few pages of the book. Check out the author's websites, blogs, etc.

You may also find reviews on blog posts, YouTube, etc.

(If an author or publisher sends you a review copy - that's different to buying a review. For example, you are not obliged to review the book on Amazon and can review on your blog, etc., not "encouraged" to leave a 5-star review, no financial incentive, etc. In this situation, you may wish to declare in your review that you were sent a review copy!)

When writing a review yourself - try to be constructive. If the book didn't get 5 stars - what could that book have done to get an extra book? What would you have liked to see within the book that was missing? Which parts of the book did you find most valuable/interesting?

If you've read a great book, why not write a review of your own? Either as a blog post, video, social media post, or the website you purchased the book. This could help others when deciding whether to read a book.

Reading Hints & Tips

Finding time to read

I think many of us have been guilty of this - we buy a new book, get excited about reading it, yet other things distract us, and the book sits on the bookshelf never to be read! **What do I think is the best way to find time to read?**

- **Will the book help your work?** Rather than thinking about the book as something to read outside of work, consider it **part of your working day**, and make time accordingly.

- **Consider how much of a difference the book will make.** If you plan on carrying out any action after reading a non-fiction book - do it!

- **Do you really need to watch the latest episode of "I'm A Celebrity"?** Or look at your Facebook every hour? Have an evening where you switch your phone off or leave it in another room, and use that time to read a book.

- Not something I've tried myself (yet!) - **listen to audio books while you work or carry out other tasks.**

- **Start reading the book, and read a chapter - or even just a page.** Once you start, you'll read more than you realised.

- **Don't feel like you have to spend hours a day reading a book.** Even just half an hour. Or 10 minutes and a few pages.

- **Don't rush - especially with non-fiction.** Take time to absorb the information, carrying out the steps, etc. rather than trying to quickly read the entire book.

- **Alternatively you may find it easier to clear an afternoon in your diary to read.** As previously mentioned, don't rush - take your time, write notes, etc.

Take a break

You don't have to constantly read book after book. In the past, I've gone a few months between reading (and rereading) different books - and it's not hurt my business. Some business owners have never read a business book!

Perhaps you just choose to read one book. Or you want some time to reflect on the ideas on the previous book you have just read.

You may not even want to think about non-fiction books and their ideas for a while - and this is perfectly normal.

You don't have to read one book, put it down, and immediately pick up the next book. You may even want to take a break between reading a book, before reading that book again and/or trying the ideas within their pages.

There may be particular times of the year when you find yourself reading more - e.g. sitting outside reading during Summer - or enjoying the nice weather and staying indoors to read during Winter.

Have some time away from non-fiction and business books - read some fiction books instead, watch Netflix, and have some time away from your business and reading non-fiction books.

Note down any key ideas or interesting points - although not so much that you become overwhelmed or lose track of the really important parts.

Read a great book? Don't put it on your bookcase!

Have you just read a really great non-fiction book? Have you even considered making changes to your business, carrying out actions, etc. from the book? And then placed the book on your bookcase, never to be read again?

- Keep the book next to your chair or desk if it helps - always on standby to reread.

- Go back to particular chapters - even reread a page, to help remind yourself of what you have learned.

- If you didn't write notes the first time round, reread the book - take your time and write notes.

- Have you read any of the author's other books? Could they prove just as valuable?

- Follow the author on Twitter, Facebook and/or LinkedIn if they have profiles on their websites. Subscribe to their newsletter if they have one.

- Visit their website - read their blogs, watch any videos they have posted, subscribe to their podcast, and download any extra content.

- Write a review of the book! Whether it's in the Amazon listing, your own blog or within my business book Facebook group.

- If it helps, add a note to your diary, phone calendar or to-do list to revisit the book at a later date.

If you read the book, and you are going to take action - then don't just say you are, and actually do it! Carry out any steps - try things mentioned in the book - reread sections - and don't just put the book away and then forget about it.

Why I don't own many business books

The heading may sound like an unusual thing for someone who organises a book group (and writing this book) to say!

However, looking through my collection of business related books I don't actually own that many. The ones I do have are often from the same authors too. That is not necessarily a bad thing!

While it's good to read different business books, I think it's also important to re-read and implement the steps in the books that I've already read. I'll often go back to particular sections, revisit chapters, write notes and take my time implementing the steps.

No point in reading a book if I put it away and forget about it. Or say "I'm going to do stuff" as a result of reading the book, and again not doing anything.

If I've found a book to be particularly valuable, I will often check out and read other books the author has written. I'll also follow them on Twitter, check out their blog posts, etc.

I'm also quite picky when it comes to reading a book - I won't purchase or read a book just because "it's in fashion" or I don't think I'm going to get anything from it.

Saying that, I have discovered some excellent new books to read - whether that is through recommendations, browsing the bookshops, or ones I've discovered in charity shops.

Whether you've only read one business book, or hundreds - the numbers don't really matter - what is important is that you have actually read and gained something from the books.

How many books do you read a year?

How many books did you read during the previous year? Was it more than - less - around the same as previous years - or perhaps you didn't read any books?

Some experts advise to read a book every week - however I don't believe that necessarily means reading 52 books a year.

The important part is reading - rather than necessarily rushing to read 52 books!

In the previous section I mentioned I don't actually own that many business books - I prefer to revisit books I've previously read - find things I missed originally and trying the steps - rather than constantly reading new books and putting back on the bookcase.

If you want to read 52 books, 12, 10, 5 or even just one during this year - that's great!

(If it is just one book - remember that one is still better than zero!)

The key thing is you are reading and getting something from those books - actually learning something, trying what you read (rather than saying "I'm going to do this!" and then completely forgetting or losing enthusiasm) - it actually helps move your business forward.

Don't just reading something to tick off a weekly task or to rush reading the entire book - take your time, read the book properly, reflect, absorb the information, learn and try new ideas.

Spending a few weeks reading one book can be more effective then rushing to read the book in one week.

Everyone is different though - some may enjoy and like to read a new book every week (especially with audiobooks which you can have in the background while you work) while others may prefer to stick to their favourites. Try and do what works for you.

It really doesn't matter how many books you read a year - as long as you are reading, learning and actually doing something about it.

The other question I could ask - how many new books do you read or plan to read?

There is nothing wrong with not buying, borrowing or reading a new book for months or even a year - and instead rereading some of the books you have already read.

Although I will say it's still a great idea to try and read books from other authors - you may discover another must-read author or book that you will continue to revisit.

While I'm always looking for ideas for new books to read, I have a favourite set of books and authors I'm always rereading (whether that's the entire book or just going back to a page or chapter) and trying what the book covers - not just trying it once, but actually taking my time to try the steps.

And if you don't like the commitment of reading an entire book - find a book where it's easy to refer to particular chapters, read blogs, listen to podcasts, etc. - there are so many options and possibilities.

It really is a case of quality over quantity!

Shortcuts

Sometimes it can feel difficult to find time to read, or we may be "too busy".

As with most things, there are not really any shortcuts when it comes to learning new skills or reading non-fiction - you are not going to become an expert overnight.

Here are some shortcuts and time saving tips...

- **Follow the author and look at their YouTube videos, Facebook, Twitter and website.** Many authors share hints and tips, examples and ideas from their books.

- **Audiobooks while you work.** Audiobooks are great to have in the background, while you work and carry out other tasks.

- **Find books with short chapters and sections.** There are many books with short chapters and sections - where you can just read the parts most relevant or of interest to you, or take your time reading a few pages every day.

- **Reading doesn't always have to be books.** Find podcasts, blog posts or magazines relevant to your business.

- **Pick a "book of the year".** One or two books that you will read and focus on for the next 12 months - allowing plenty of time to implement and try the ideas within the book.

- **Don't feel like reading at the moment?** It's perfectly normal to have a break from reading business books - and do something else. You can go back to reading again when you are ready, or find the right book for you.

- **Combine with your other business activities.** I'm not just talking about trying the ideas and steps in the book. For example, are you looking for something to share on your social media? Add a post about the book you are reading!

- **Who are your favourite business leaders?** Read their books and biographies - may feel less like work, while still gaining some inspiration.

- **Remember it's not about reading 52 books a year.** Someone can read one book a year, and take a lot of action, compared to someone reading 52 books and quickly moving on to the next book without taking any real action.

- **Join a book club and find the right books for you.** I'm not just saying this because of my own book group! Finding ideas from what others are reading is not only a great way of finding motivation to read, you can save a lot of time reading bad books, as others will recommend books.

- **Speed reading.** Not a tactic I've tried myself, and requires a bit of skill (there are entire books written on this subject)!

Some of these may not be real shortcuts, however they will save time and make reading non-fiction books much easier.

You'll get the full advantages of reading a book, by reading the actual book. However, some of these shortcuts are ideal if you are unsure about reading a particular book, or looking to revisit ideas that you have already read.

As with all things - don't cut corners. Take your time to read, it can be more effective to read a few pages, then try the ideas you have just read about, rather than rushing to read the complete book.

There are no quick fixes. If you are reading a book to help address a challenge within your business, it will take time (and if you need urgent help, then perhaps it's worth seeking professional advice).

Yes, you have lots of work and projects you need to do. However, learning new skills and reading non-fiction books - which in the long-run will help your business - is part of your working day, rather than something you need to find time for separately.

You don't have to read an entire book - pick the chapters that are of most interest or relevance to you.

Read one page

We've all been guilty of buying at least one book at some point, which we keep meaning to read, and never actually even looking at again. Every time we see the book, it's a case of "getting round to reading it at some point" - even setting a day where we'll read and then getting distracted by other things.

Sometimes we may feel that we are "too busy" to read a book.

The example I often use is people saying they don't have time to read, yet manage to rewatch every episode of Game Of Thrones (sometimes twice!). Or the latest episodes of a TV soap.

(And a lot of the time not really watching those TV shows, and just browsing the Internet on the phone).

One of my favourite reading tips is to just read one page of a book. You don't have to read the rest of the book, or even a chapter - just pick up the book and read a page.

You may even find yourself reading more than one page. Or even the entire book!

You don't even have to read the beginning - find a section that is most interesting for you.

Don't rush reading a book, take your time, write notes and actually try the steps.

Not rushing and reading a chapter a time, or a few pages - also provides a good opportunity to reflect on what you have just read.

It's easy to read lots and lots of books, and then never try anything from the books - while you may read a few pages, try the steps and take more action as a result.

Here's a tactic I use... next to my sofa I have a pile of books (they never sit on a bookcase as frequently re-read and revisit them). When I'm bored or have a spare minute, instead of reaching for my phone, I'll pick up one of the books and read a few pages - or even a chapter. I may even decide that instead of what I'd originally planned, I'll continue reading the book instead.

(The above photo is actually the pile of books next to my sofa - that sit on a chair that is very rarely used as a chair!)

Try this yourself - keep a few books nearby - and during the ad breaks for your favourite TV shows pick up a book and read a page or two. Instead of grabbing your phone and browsing the web during a soap, look through one of the books. You may even find you prefer reading the book to watching the TV show!

Remember it's not always about reading new books every time.

Make it a goal to read one page of a book every day.

Perhaps as time goes on, increase that goal to a few more pages, or even an entire chapter (although you may find yourself reading more than one page once you start reading anyway)!

Seeing a book and the idea of reading a few hundred pages may put you off - however you don't have to read the entire book in one day (or even in one week or month). Take your time and as long as you need to read the book.

As well as ideas for books to read that you may not have considered, book clubs are a great way of providing accountability, meeting new people and networking.

Reading physical or Kindle books is not the only option - there are audiobooks that you can listen to while you carry out other tasks.

There are also magazines, trade publications, etc. that you can read to help improve your work or business.

And while not strictly books - podcasts and reading blog posts are a great way of finding out what is happening in your industry, learning new skills and discovering new ideas that you can try yourself.

Finally - it's tempting to consider reading as something extra - however consider taking some time to read as part of your working day. Set yourself an hour, half an hour - or even 5 or 10 minutes - to read.

Random pages

A technique I often use - especially if I have a few minutes - **grab a book, open the book at a random page, and read that page.**

(If it's in the middle of a section or chapter, you can either start from where you end up, or go to the start of that particular section!)

Sometimes it may be something new, or a part of the book you have read before. **Just open the book, and see where you end up!**

It's something that can be used alongside the other ideas I've shared here. It's a bit like grabbing a phone when we are bored, although reading a few pages from a book instead of scrolling! And like with scrolling, you can end up reading more than you intended.

You can either do this with a book on top of your pile of books, or select a random book.

It's a technique I often use– either with new books, or books I've previously read. Occasionally I've tried this technique so many times with a particular book, I've ended up reading that entire book!

Although it is still effective to read a book from start to end - this is a great technique to use if you want to revisit a book you've read, or find the idea of reading an entire book overwhelming.

It's similar to how we browse in bookstores and discover new books, we may open a random page, and see if we like it. However, it's with books we already own, and in a bit more detail.

Let your curiosity take control, and guide you!

Taking Action

Can business books achieve your goals?

Can reading business or personal development books help you achieve your plans and goals? The short answer is possibly!

For a start, it can depend on the goal - for example learning a new skill, focusing on improving a particular area of your business, mindset, etc.

It's not just work - there are personal goals you may wish to achieve.

(Although in some cases, e.g. health, remember that reading non-fiction books is never a substitute for seeking professional or medical advice.)

As with all things, remember that business books are not a magic solution that will instantly solve everything.

Trying the ideas within their pages can (and will) take time. You can't just read the book, put it back on the bookcase, and expect things to magically happen on their own.

Even with inspirational or motivational books, you still need to take action.

Reading a book may not be the only solution - and picking a few non-fiction books to help you with your goals, is something to do alongside other tools, help, and resources.

No book can offer a quick fix, make you a millionaire overnight, or help you "get rich quick". If a book makes such promises, be careful. While profits/sales may be your ultimate goal, thinking about money may also effect how you approach a book you are reading.

If you are really struggling with your business - books are not the answer, and never a substitute for seeking professional help/advice.

Decide on what you goals will be - perhaps break them down into smaller goals. What will you need to learn? What action do you need to take? And find suitable books to help with this (and of course my book group can also help you find suitable books).

A lot of people use January/new year to set goals - however if that's a few months from now, don't use it as an excuse to delay - start now.

Remember there is 12 months in a year - a new year isn't just January. Some goals may even take longer to achieve or see results - and something to continue working on into the following year and beyond.

Ways to take action

Throughout this book, I often talk about writing notes, trying ideas, etc. - however there are a few ways you can take action from a book you've read…

- Reflect on their words.
- Try the ideas within their pages.
- Write notes as you read the books.
- Mix of all of these.
- Do nothing! Yes, this really is an option.

Some may be more appropriate depending on the type of book you are reading - for example, a biography may inspire you, and you wish to reflect on their words. While with a practical "how to" book you might write notes and try some of the ideas.

You may be looking for motivation or inspiration - and at other times you may be looking for more practical steps you can try.

Remember business books are something you can use alongside other resources - e.g. local Business Gateway help, etc.

Something I've said throughout these pages - take your time! A few days, weeks or even months - trying one or two ideas at a time, or reading a chapter and reflecting rather than trying to read the whole book in one go.

Stop at any point and try/reflect - even if you are halfway through a chapter and it feels appropriate.

If you only want to reflect and consider what you've just read, that's normal. You don't always have to roll up your sleeves and take action.

Don't immediately forget what you have just read. Perhaps go for a walk, or something else that's not too distracting and allows time for you to reflect on a book's words.

Even if it's a more practical book - you may want to spend some time considering whether it's appropriate for your business, and how you will apply those ideas yourself.

You may also find it helpful to re-read a particular paragraph or section half an hour or a day or two later.

While notes are great, don't write so many notes you become overwhelmed. Note a few ideas, or use a post-it note. You could have the book next to you while trying ideas, or bookmark important parts to go back to later. You could note page numbers you want to return to, instead of detailed notes.

Sometimes you could find yourself trying the ideas, taking steps, etc. without realising, even if it's not something you noted down or thought was important initially.

Having an initial spark of inspiration is great - however whether you reflect on the words, or carry out more practical action - the key point here is to take some form of action!

If you are thinking of trying something - there's a good chance you should go for it (as long as you don't end up bankrupt or in debt!) - get a basic version working!

Don't follow a business book!

Business and personal development books are a great way of developing and learning new skills - however that doesn't mean you should always follow them word-for-word!

I've often mentioned people not actually trying the ideas within non-fiction books. While this section may contradict this a little bit - there is a difference between trying the ideas blindly, and actually making them work for you.

Would I encourage you to try the ideas within a book you have read? Yes! Should you follow a book blindly, without questioning or adapting the ideas? No, absolutely not.

I can often spot businesses that have obviously read particular books - e.g. businesses pretending to have limited capacities. If I've seen through these tactics, so can other people - even someone who doesn't read any books.

Make up your own mind. Adapt the ideas for what works for your business. Pick and mix what works for you. And don't be afraid to challenge the ideas.

Take a recipe in a cooking book. Don't have sunflower oil? Use vegetable oil instead! Prefer adding cranberries instead of sultanas? Then go ahead and change them. Want to add chocolate chips to plain cookies? Go ahead! In fact, eventually, the recipe may stop being the original, and become your own unique creation.

(With recipes, it's also worth remembering that despite the well-known name on the book cover, most recipes when taken to their basic versions, are identical or variations of other recipes.)

It's tempting to follow a book word-for-word - especially from a well-known author. However, those are ideas that have worked for them (or worse in some cases ideas they have just written and never really done themselves). They got to where they are, because they made up their own minds on things, tried different ideas, etc.

And they probably didn't get it perfect every time - with every success - there are 10 times the things that didn't work out perfectly.

Don't try everything in a book in one go either. Reread and revisit a book. Try one of two ideas, and get them working really well. And go back and try something else.

Just because a book said you can't do something, doesn't mean it can't be tried within your own business (as long as you are not financially ruining yourself).

Different business books may even contradict each other. Pick and mix ideas from different books that you like. Don't let doubt get in your way.

Disagree with something written in a book? That's normal too - you are not going to agree with everyone - not even your best friend. If you disagree with an idea, don't rule out other ideas within a book.

Unsure about an idea? Discuss with other business owners (not armchair experts)! Perhaps join a book club, where you can discuss what works and what doesn't.

A lot of books will contain some really good ideas, plus some ideas you don't want to try or won't agree with - and this is normal.

You may have found a book to be a great read, and then changed your mind later on upon reflection. You may also not have got anything from a book when initially reading, however it has proven more valuable when you re-read and revisit a book.

I've also seen many "experts" share advice and guidance that is actually bad practice - or worse breaks terms and conditions of other websites - both online in groups and blogs - but also in some business books too.

Don't be afraid to verify any ideas or facts in any book you read. I could claim to be a popstar on this page of this book - however doesn't mean it's true!

Just because you have read a book, doesn't mean you have to try every single idea within their pages.

While grand ideas are great - don't spend money that you don't really have.

If there are problems within your business, don't constantly read business books, hoping SOMETHING will work. If you are really struggling, you may wish to seek professional advice.

Unless you are reading a book on brain surgery - however even then you would probably learn a bit more before actually carrying out surgery on someone!

Business books can be really valuable for your business - with ideas that will prove valuable. That doesn't mean you have to follow ideas word-for-word - especially when they get in the way of progress or stop your business growing.

Ideas are exactly that - ideas! Try, challenge, adapt, and disagree...

How business books are similar to recipe books

Look carefully at a lot of recipes - whether online, from celebrity chefs, etc. - you'll find that recipes (especially when taken to their basic steps/ingredients) are essentially the same.

As an example, look at and compare a Mary Berry, Nigella or Paul Hollywood cake recipe - it's still flour, eggs, sugar and butter. The same basic recipe as any other cake recipe! If you have a recipe book nearby grab a few and look for similar cakes - or look online - and compare them.

There's only so many ways you can make a cake.

It's the same with business books - a lot of books may not have radical new ideas - or have the classic ideas that have worked for businesses over the years (perhaps exaggerated and made to look like the author's own ideas).

Sometimes you want to remove the author's own "radical" aspects, and get down to the very basics of the idea or technique. On other occasions, you may want to read the ideas presented in different ways, and with different viewpoints. You may just enjoy the author's own take or insights into something.

Like a recipe for a cake that seems a challenge - you may either enjoy the challenge of making the cake (at least you tried, and I'm sure it will be delicious, even if it doesn't look like the photo in the book!) or look for a cake recipe that's more realistic to try - the same principles apply to business books.

The ideas you read or try don't always have to be radical, a lot of time the classic and more traditional ways will be exactly what you are looking for.

Just one idea

You may have heard of "the one thing" - here's a variation of that…

Some books will have lots of ideas - whether that's creating lots of assets or following some exercises to improve your mindset. Don't feel like you have to try EVERYTHING in the book.

Pick just one idea from the books you have recently read.

Only one idea. Pick that idea, and spend some time - it could even be a few months - and focus on trying that idea really well.

Focus exclusively on that idea. Forget all the other ideas in the book's 100+ pages for now, if you can (and if you can't - are you sure that you can't?)

The one idea could make a big difference to your business.

It could be an idea you particularly love, or feel will make a difference - you don't have to justify why you've picked that idea - the most important thing is you have picked one.

Even if you feel the idea will only make a small difference for your business, it will still build and add up.

So which ONE IDEA from a book you have recently read will you pick and focus on?

Pick one idea - only one - from a book you have read. Spend some time focusing on trying that idea really well. Don't try everything in one go.

Don't depend on business books

While reading non-fiction books can make a difference, and give you new ideas to try - don't rely on them.

Use the ideas and what you learn from these books alongside other tools, techniques, resources and help.

Just because a business book recommends something different to how you are currently doing things doesn't necessarily mean you have to get rid of your current setup. You can disagree with what a book says - or even mix ideas together.

You may also find ideas from a book don't necessarily work for your business or current situation, although still worthwhile trying.

Beware of books encouraging you to spend lots of money with the author's consultancy, services, etc.

Don't spend so much time trying the ideas that you forget why you started your business in the first place, or that you lose your vision.

If you are struggling in your business - e.g. you are not making any money, etc. - business books may not necessarily be the answer.

Getting the most from books you read

A lot of people read non-fiction books once - put them away and never actually do anything or re-read the book. Sometimes people will buy a book, and never get round to reading a single page!

So what do I think is the best way to take full advantage of the books you read?

- Follow the steps in the book - if it asks you to write stuff down or stop and think, then take some time to do that.

- Have you ever read a book, think "I'm going to take a lot of action" and never do anything? I think we've all been guilty of that at one point or another. Revisit the book, re-read, go back to previous sections, take notes, etc.

- Everyone is different. While it's good to discover new books, I have a favourite set of books I re-read and revisit regularly.

- If placing a book on your bookcase means they are forgotten, leave them on your desk instead. Have them where they are easy to grab and revisit.

- Don't rush and read one book, and immediately move on to book after book, without absorbing the information.

- Don't enjoy reading a book or find it difficult to follow? There is one well-known and widely recommended book (which will remain nameless!) that I struggled to read, did not enjoy reading, so I moved on to something else. Don't feel like you have to read the book, or complete the book if you don't get anything out of it.

- If there is a particular book or author you like, follow them on social media, check out their blogs, and have a look at their other books.

The most important thing - if you think the book has good ideas - make sure you actually carry them out.

Don't give up!

It's tempting to throw in the towel and give up at the first obstacle - whether it's a book you are not enjoying, or ideas that don't work out.

Keep going!

Adapt and try the ideas in a different way, learning more about the topic, or finding a different book that you actually enjoy reading.

I've mentioned earlier that reading business/personal development books, while work related, should still be something that you enjoy.

Look at your approach, experiment, and try ideas differently.

So many read a book and say it "didn't work" - sometimes it's not a great book, other times they just didn't do anything about what they actually read. Remember that things don't magically happen just by holding a book in your hands or looking at the front cover!

I've read books in the past where I didn't agree, went back and enjoyed reading the second time around - or found myself trying the ideas without even realising it! Perhaps take a break.

Change takes time - with pretty much any part of your business, you can't do something and expect instant results - it may take a few days, weeks, or even years!

Have you tried the ideas in the books you have read? Are you sure? And did you give up when they didn't work out at the first attempt?

You've just read a book - what's next?

Once you've read a business or personal development book, here's what you could do next...

- **Follow the author on social media** - connect with them on LinkedIn, like their Facebook page, join their groups, follow on Twitter, etc.
- **Subscribe to the author's newsletter** if they have one!
- **Check out the authors blog posts.**
- **Send a message to the author letting them know how the book helped you.**
- **Revisit particular sections and chapters.**
- **Write notes and take action.**
- **Looked at the author's other books.**
- **Shared a review - either in a book group, on Amazon, as a blog post, video or on social media.**
- **Talk about the book you've read at a book club meeting!**

Remember - reading a book is not a race. Don't just read a book, and immediately forget about it and move on to the next one.

Take your time, learn from the books and implement those changes that you promised yourself while reading the book!

And as I've mentioned throughout this book - just because you have read a book doesn't mean you can put it away. Go back, briefly (or in more detail!) go back and look at sections of the book you have just read, and pick a few ideas to try.

More Hints & Tips

To end this section of the book (and the book itself) - here's a round-up of some of my favourite book reading hints and tips...

- **Check out the author's website, Facebook groups and blogs.** Not only is it a great way to interact with the author and get additional material - authors sometimes make their books available for free, make worksheets available to help you implement steps in the book, organise workshops or have sample or extra book content that you can read.

- **Purchased a book? Share a photo and post on Facebook (including my book group!), LinkedIn and Twitter.** On one occasion, I posted about a book I found on a charity shop, and the post ended up going a bit viral!

- **Follow the author on LinkedIn, Twitter, etc.** Authors will often share hints, tips and news on their books or events.

- **Check out your local library.** Some libraries even have ebooks available that you can download for free from their website using your library card.

- **Keep books next to your chair or sofa.** This is something I do - rather than reaching for a phone when I have a few minutes, I'll reach for a book and read a few pages!

- **You don't have to read lots of books.** Some coaches and consultants recommend reading 52 books a year (or a book a week) - however it can be more effective to go back to books you have previously read.

- **Take your time.** You don't have to read a book in one go. Whether it's a few pages, an entire chapter or even one page.

- **Write your own book!** If you think you can do better than the authors you are reading, why not share your own experiences and write/self publish your own book?

- **Looking for ideas for books to read?** Look in my book group, ask online for recommendations, consider what you are looking for help with or to improve at the moment, or read books by your favourite authors or public figures.

- **Choose a format that works well for you.** Whether that's paperback, audiobooks, ebooks or even a mixture.

- **Some services offer summaries of books, however I have mixed views on these.** Sometimes it can be better to just read the original book. The most notable one is Blinkist - however with many of these services the original author's don't get paid as they are just summaries of work. If you use these services, find one that involves the original book authors.

- **Look at book reviews.** Be aware that some reviews (especially on Amazon) are written by the author's clients, family and friends. Not just on Amazon - you can often find reviews on blogs, websites and social media. I often write and share reviews of books I've read on LinkedIn.

- **Struggle to find the time to read? Consider taking half an hour or so to read as part of your working day, rather than something extra you have to do.** Try and find the time to read - even if it means watching fewer episodes in your Game Of Thrones marathon!

- **Even if you believe you know everything, there is still something to learn.** Whether that's books you maybe ruled out because you are already an expert on that subject, or chapters you read and didn't really make use of.

Don't wait until tomorrow or for the "perfect" moment (you'll keep putting it off). Pick up a book NOW and start reading - even one page.

The above paragraph/statement also applies to taking action from books you have read.

Many of these have been covered in greater detail throughout this book.

Having a sudden burst of inspiration after reading a book is the easy part - however are you actually going to do anything about it?

Book Clubs

There are many business book clubs now - many have a particular book, while others (including my own) discuss what everyone's reading at the moment.

Have a look and see if there are any business book clubs in your local area - you may also find some national groups via Zoom.

Book groups are a great place to discuss the books you are reading, and finding ideas for new books to read. There are also great opportunities for networking - meeting (and getting to know) other business owners, and catching up with existing contacts.

They can provide a sense of accountability - not just reading the books, actually discussing the ideas you have tried, asking for help from other people, how the ideas have worked, etc.

If a book club doesn't exist in your area - why not start your own?

My own business book group is based in Aberdeen, although in addition to meetings there is a Facebook group that welcomes members from other parts of the UK. You can find more info on my book group at: www.booksandnetworking.co.uk

Think you can do better?

Ever read a book (or done anything else) and thought that you could do a better job?

You have knowledge, skills and experience that you will have built up over the years - real world experience that could help other business owners. So if you think you can do better - why not write your own book?

Start as blog posts that you'll eventually collect into a book, or write a few ideas at a time - if you want to write your own book, go for it.

Don't write a book as a glorified business card, or because you believe you'll "get rich quick" - that's how it will come across to readers, even if you don't realise it. Don't be tempted to cut corners by using AI or releasing so-called "low content books" either.

Write about what you have knowledge and enthusiasm for - don't worry too much about niches, formatting, etc. - the first step is to write your ideas down. Worry about formatting, self publishing, etc. later.

(If you are interested in writing/self publishing your book - I have a book on writing/self publishing available on Amazon!)

What knowledge or skills could you pass on to other people? Do you think you can do better than the books out there at the moment, and something you have enthusiasm for and would like to share with the world?

Recommended Reading

There are many non-fiction books - and it can sometimes feel overwhelming and you may be wondering where to start.

As this is a book on reading a book, it's only appropriate I share some of my own book choices (although one of them is another book written by me)!

General Business

- **Your Product, Your Business** by Simon Pittman

- **Considering Self Employment** by Fraser Hay

- **Practical Business Coaching For The Self Employed** by Fraser Hay

- **Big Ideas for Small Businesses** by John Lamerton

- **Your Creative Business** by Angie Scarr & Kira Swales

Marketing

- **The Ultimate Small Business Marketing Book** by Dee Blick

- **How to Write Sales Letters That Sell** by Drayton Bird

- **Business Letters & Emails Made Easy** from Lawpack

- **Marketing on a Shoestring Budget** by Stuart Mason

Mindset & Motivation

- **Think Your Way To Success** by Mark Rhodes

- **Life. Business. Just Got Easier** by Brad Burton

Networking & Communication

- **How To Talk To Absolutely Anyone** by Mark Rhodes

- **Networking A Successful Small Business** by Joanne Dewberry

- **The Jelly Effect** by Andy Bounds

- **How to Succeed with People** by Paul McGee

Over time you'll soon find you have your own recommended reading list - it may be similar, or (more likely) radically different to what I've recommended here.

Why not share your own recommended reading list as a blog or social media post? If you are looking for something to blog about, reviews about particular books you have read are also great topics to write about!

And finally…

Reading non-fiction over the years has really made a difference for me - whether that's learning new skills/systems while working in IT, or growing and marketing my business.

Whether you already read business books, or you have just started reading non-fiction, I hope you enjoyed reading this book, and it helps you get the most from the books you read.

I'd love to hear your feedback - including anything you have found particularly helpful and will try yourself. It would also be great to hear how you get on trying the ideas within this book.

Send me an e-mail at **simon@libraryplayer.co.uk**

As with any other business book (and something I encourage throughout these pages) - I encourage you to revisit this book, re-read particular sections, and try some of the ideas.

And I often share blog posts on LinkedIn - including reading hints & tips and book reviews - among other things - it would be great to connect with you at: **linkedin.com/in/SimonPittman**

Also by the author

- **Editing Audio Using Audacity**
- **Managing a WordPress Website**
- **How to Develop Software**
- **Creating A New Software Product**
- **Writing & Self Publishing Your Book**
- **Your Product, Your Business**

All the above books are available on Amazon!